Get ready to conquer the next 12 weeks.

Copyright and Permissions

TABLE OF CONTENTS

ORIENTATION

This isn't your mama's day planner. Living life to the fullest is more than knowing what time you're meeting friends for drinks. To live your best life, you need focus and purpose, a sense of moving forward, and time for the things you love. I never found a planner that gave me a way to capture that in a single place, so I set out to create the perfect one. And the Life-Hacking Day Tracker was born!

This action map is only 12 weeks long because (as you've probably noticed) life is constantly throwing us curve balls. Where we are and what we need can vary so much throughout the course of a full year. By simply focusing a few months at a time, you will better stay on track. And with Life-Hacking Day Tracker Review & Plan sessions, each month will be better than the last.

Be sure to check out www.caseyjourdan.com to find more inspiration and life hacks.

THE PROCESS

FIRST, on pages 7-9, you'll get clear on your visions: what drives you and what motivates you in life.

SECOND, on pages 9-15, we will talk goals. You'll establish what you want to achieve and build a plan of action to make it really happen.

Spend time on these first two sections. Pour a cup of your favorite tea or coffee, flip on some tunes, and snuggle in. This is the base work for the entire planner. These parts are also what make this guide so much more than just another planner.

THIRD, there are three full-month calendar spreads. I've designed this planner with no dates, so you can start whenever is right for you. This is a great place to put in birthdays, vacation days, and other big events. This is your fast view of the month ahead.

FOURTH, right after each full-month spread are the Review + Plan pages. This is your chance to look back on the last month and see what worked. Then, take some time to look at the month ahead. This is how you make sure you're still on track with your visions and goals. Taking the time to focus on these pages every month will make the next 12 weeks more productive than ever before.

LAST are your daily planner pages.
There are two parts here:

1. Every lifestyle guru and mega-moneymaker swears by starting the day with their variation of a brain dump. I've created a day-hack page so you easily do the same.

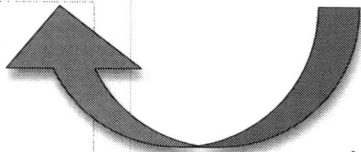

Take a few minutes to get clear on your top three focuses for the day. Get your stress out of your head and onto paper where you can leave it behind, then focus on what you're grateful for.

The example planner form shows:

Date: 2/18   SUN MON TUE WED THU FRI SAT

Top 3 focuses today
1. Clean the kitchen
2. Get a workout!
3. Pack for weekend away!

What's got you stressed?   Stress: Low Medium High

I'm sooo behind on the Smith project!

What are you grateful for?

Today I'm grateful for weekend's away with friends and laughing til my face hurts.

Water
XX XX
X

Don't-Forgets!
Don't forget to call Hailey when I'm on my way!

2. Your actual schedule. There are no times, so you can break down your day in the way that suits you.

NOTE: Don't be overwhelmed by all these extra things to track. Research is proving time and again that the people who are tuned into the details in life are the happiest and most productive.

Checking in with your goals on a routine basis and being aware of your life, your stressors, and gratitudes are the foundations for living life fully.

The example schedule form shows:

Morning
meeting w/ team

Notes
Bring COFFEE!

Mid-Day
noon - lunch and learn meeting
2:00 - call w/ west coast team

Call m @ 801-001-1234

Evening
7:00 - drinks w/ sweetie

Now for the hopes, dreams, and unicorns.

What are three things you want to focus on for the next 12 weeks?

1.

2.

3.

What are three promises you are making to yourself for the next 12 weeks?

1.

2.

3.

VISION

This planner is more than just tracking what time lunch is and which weekend you're going to visit your parents. This planner goes one step further and becomes your guide for getting focused, taking action, and making change in your life.

Fill out the next few pages thinking about the answers to those two questions asked on the previous page. What do you want, or *need*, to achieve in the next 12 weeks?

Don't just focus on work goals either. Think about your relationships with family and friends, or about taking steps toward that pie-in-the-sky dream of yours. Remember the saying "The journey of a thousand miles begins with a single step"? This planner is your road map to those first few steps.

VISION

Don't overthink these questions, don't censor yourself, and remember that there are no wrong answers.

1. What are the 10 things you enjoy doing most?

2. What are three things you must do every day to feel complete?

3. What five values do you consider most important?

4. If you never had to work again, what would you spend your days doing?

Now write a short paragraph: your personal vision statement, fully articulating what you want for your future. Vision statements can change with time, so don't fear being trapped or obligated to what you write now.

GOALS

Next up is goal setting. One of the key reasons we don't achieve our goals is that we don't write them down. We set a far-reaching goal but make no plan for how to actually achieve it. Then in six months or a year, we're mad at ourselves for failing.

You're going to start with the goal then begin building the path to succeed at that goal. You should work through this process for each major goal you have. Photocopy the next three pages as many times as necessary.

Let's Make It Happen

What is your pie-in-the-sky goal?

Being inspired by your goal is of vital importance. Describe what it will look like when you achieve this goal. What will it feel like? I want you to know **why** this goal matters to you. Get specific.

Action Plan

Now for the part of goal setting that most people skip: the plan of action.

First, set a deadline. It does *not* have to be in the next 12 weeks. Be honest and realistic. When are you going to achieve this big goal? _____

Second, what steps can you take in the next 12 weeks to move you toward completing your goal? These may be mini-goals and milestones or daily and weekly tasks. If you're stuck, work backward and start breaking large steps into little, more manageable ones. Keep in mind that these should be **actions**; this is the "doing" part that makes the big goal achievable.

Brainstorm here. Just get it out of your head. We'll organize in a moment.

Laying It All Out

Take all the pieces from the previous page and start putting them in order. Build your action plan for the next 12 weeks. There is space on the next page too.

Lastly, plug all this into your calendar and get to work!

Dates, to-dos, & gratitudes. Schedule life here.

SUNDAY	MONDAY	TUESDAY	WEDNESDAY
____	____	____	____
____	____	____	____
____	____	____	____
____	____	____	____
____	____	____	____

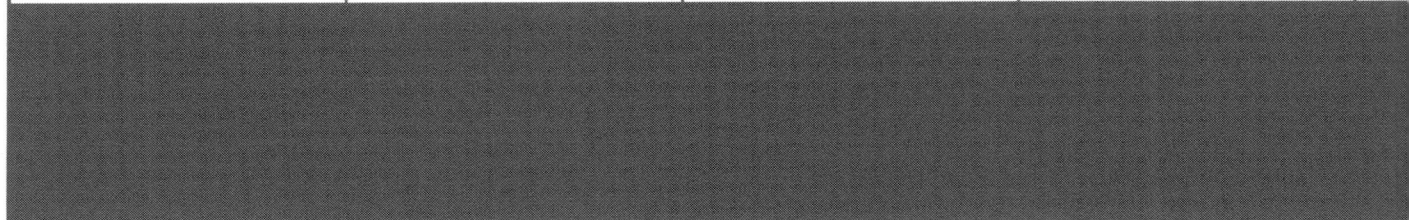

THURSDAY	FRIDAY	SATURDAY	NOTES

MONTH

REVIEW

Look back on the last 30 days and answer the following:

What was fun, fulfilling, or just worked really, really well?

What could have gone better? No judgment, simply a chance to reflect.

What do you want to make more time for next month?
What do you want to spend less time doing?

What areas of life in the past 30 days felt too complicated?
Where could you benefit from less chaos?

How can you simplify these areas in the next 30 days?

PLAN

What two things do you want to focus on during the next 30 days?

1.

2.

What are you procrastinating on right now? Is this because of fear or lack of skill?

How are you going to overcome this?

What steps do you need to take in order to implement your answers from the previous page? Get those things on (or off) the calendar for next month.

Review your Goals & Visions pages. Make sure the steps you need to be taking are scheduled. If you need to adjust the timeline on your goals, now is the time.

Go forth and conquer the next 30 days.

Date: _____   SUN MON TUE WED THU FRI SAT

Top three focuses today

1. _____

2. _____

3. _____

What's got you stressed?   Now let it go.

What are you **grateful** for?

Water

Don't-Forgets!

Morning

Notes

Mid-Day

Evening

Date: _____   SUN MON TUE WED THU FRI SAT

Top three focuses today

1. _____

2. _____

3. _____

What's got you stressed?   Now let it go.

What are you **grateful** for?

Water

Don't-Forgets!

Morning

Notes

Mid-Day

Evening

Date: _____   SUN MON TUE WED THU FRI SAT

Top three focuses today

1. _____

2. _____

3. _____

What's got you stressed?   Now let it go.

What are you **grateful** for?

Water

Don't-Forgets!

Morning

Notes

Mid-Day

Evening

Date: _____   SUN MON TUE WED THU FRI SAT

Top three focuses today

1. _____

2. _____

3. _____

What's got you stressed?   Now let it go.

What are you **grateful** for?

Water

Don't-Forgets!

Morning

Notes

Mid-Day

Evening

Date: _____   SUN MON TUE WED THU FRI SAT

Top three focuses today

1. _____

2. _____

3. _____

What's got you stressed?   Now let it go.

What are you **grateful** for?

Water   **Don't-Forgets!**

Morning

Notes

Mid-Day

Evening

Date: _____   SUN MON TUE WED THU FRI SAT

Top three focuses today

1. _____

2. _____

3. _____

What's got you stressed?   Now let it go.

What are you **grateful** for?

Water

Don't-Forgets!

Morning

Notes

Mid-Day

Evening

Date: _____ SUN MON TUE WED THU FRI SAT

Top three focuses today

1. _____

2. _____

3. _____

What's got you stressed?   Now let it go.

What are you **grateful** for?

Water

Don't-Forgets!

Morning

Notes

Mid-Day

Evening

Date: _____   SUN MON TUE WED THU FRI SAT

Top three focuses today

1. _____

2. _____

3. _____

What's got you stressed?   Now let it go.

What are you **grateful** for?

Water

Don't-Forgets!

Morning

Notes

Mid-Day

Evening

Date: _____   SUN MON TUE WED THU FRI SAT

Top three focuses today

1. _____

2. _____

3. _____

What's got you stressed?   Now let it go.

What are you **grateful** for?

Water

Don't-Forgets!

Morning

Notes

Mid-Day

Evening

Date: _____   SUN MON TUE WED THU FRI SAT

Top three focuses today

1. _____

2. _____

3. _____

What's got you stressed?   Now let it go.

What are you **grateful** for?

Water

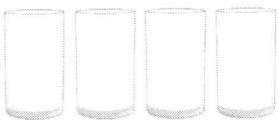

Don't-Forgets!

Morning

Notes

Mid-Day

Evening

Date: _____   SUN MON TUE WED THU FRI SAT

Top three focuses today

1. _____

2. _____

3. _____

What's got you stressed?   Now let it go.

What are you **grateful** for?

Water

Don't-Forgets!

Morning

Notes

Mid-Day

Evening

Date: _____   SUN MON TUE WED THU FRI SAT

Top three focuses today

1. _____

2. _____

3. _____

What's got you stressed?   Now let it go.

What are you **grateful** for?

Water

Don't-Forgets!

Morning

Notes

Mid-Day

Evening

Date: _____   SUN MON TUE WED THU FRI SAT

Top three focuses today

1. _____

2. _____

3. _____

What's got you stressed?	Now let it go.

What are you **grateful** for?

Water

Don't-Forgets!

Morning

Notes

Mid-Day

Evening

Date: _____   SUN MON TUE WED THU FRI SAT

Top three focuses today

1. _____

2. _____

3. _____

What's got you stressed?   Now let it go.

What are you **grateful** for?

Water

Don't-Forgets!

Morning

Notes

Mid-Day

Evening

Date: _____   SUN MON TUE WED THU FRI SAT

Top three focuses today

1. _____

2. _____

3. _____

What's got you stressed?   Now let it go.

What are you **grateful** for?

Water

Don't-Forgets!

Morning

Notes

Mid-Day

Evening

Date: _____   SUN MON TUE WED THU FRI SAT

Top three focuses today

1. _____

2. _____

3. _____

What's got you stressed?   Now let it go.

What are you **grateful** for?

Water

Don't-Forgets!

Morning

Notes

Mid-Day

Evening

Date: _____   SUN MON TUE WED THU FRI SAT

Top three focuses today

1. _____

2. _____

3. _____

What's got you stressed?   Now let it go.

What are you **grateful** for?

Water

Don't-Forgets!

Morning

Notes

Mid-Day

Evening

Date: _____   SUN MON TUE WED THU FRI SAT

Top three focuses today

1. _____

2. _____

3. _____

What's got you stressed?   Now let it go.

What are you **grateful** for?

Water

Don't-Forgets!

Morning

Notes

Mid-Day

Evening

Date: _____   SUN MON TUE WED THU FRI SAT

Top three focuses today

1. _____

2. _____

3. _____

What's got you stressed?   Now let it go.

What are you **grateful** for?

Water

Don't-Forgets!

Morning

Notes

Mid-Day

Evening

Date: _____   SUN MON TUE WED THU FRI SAT

Top three focuses today

1. _____

2. _____

3. _____

What's got you stressed?   Now let it go.

What are you **grateful** for?

Water

Don't-Forgets!

Morning

Notes

Mid-Day

Evening

Date: _____   SUN MON TUE WED THU FRI SAT

Top three focuses today

1. _____

2. _____

3. _____

What's got you stressed?   Now let it go.

What are you **grateful** for?

Water

Don't-Forgets!

Morning

Notes

Mid-Day

Evening

Date: _____   SUN MON TUE WED THU FRI SAT

Top three focuses today

1. _____

2. _____

3. _____

What's got you stressed?   Now let it go.

What are you **grateful** for?

Water

Don't-Forgets!

Morning

Notes

Mid-Day

Evening

Date: _____   SUN MON TUE WED THU FRI SAT

Top three focuses today

1. _____

2. _____

3. _____

What's got you stressed?   Now let it go.

What are you **grateful** for?

Water

Don't-Forgets!

Morning

Notes

Mid-Day

Evening

Date: _____   SUN MON TUE WED THU FRI SAT

Top three focuses today

1. _____

2. _____

3. _____

What's got you stressed?   Now let it go.

What are you **grateful** for?

Water

Don't-Forgets!

Morning

Notes

Mid-Day

Evening

Date: _____   SUN MON TUE WED THU FRI SAT

Top three focuses today

1. _____

2. _____

3. _____

What's got you stressed?	Now let it go.

What are you **grateful** for?

Water

Don't-Forgets!

Morning

Notes

Mid-Day

Evening

Date: _____   SUN MON TUE WED THU FRI SAT

Top three focuses today

1. _____

2. _____

3. _____

What's got you stressed?	Now let it go.

What are you **grateful** for?

Water	Don't-Forgets!

Morning

Notes

Mid-Day

Evening

Date: _____   SUN MON TUE WED THU FRI SAT

Top three focuses today

1. _____

2. _____

3. _____

What's got you stressed?   Now let it go.

What are you **grateful** for?

Water

Don't-Forgets!

Morning

Notes

Mid-Day

Evening

Date: _____   SUN MON TUE WED THU FRI SAT

Top three focuses today

1. _____

2. _____

3. _____

What's got you stressed?   Now let it go.

What are you **grateful** for?

Water   **Don't-Forgets!**

Morning

Notes

Mid-Day

Evening

Date: _____ SUN MON TUE WED THU FRI SAT

Top three focuses today

1. _____

2. _____

3. _____

What's got you stressed?	Now let it go.

What are you **grateful** for?

Water

Don't-Forgets!

Morning

Notes

Mid-Day

Evening

Date: _____   SUN MON TUE WED THU FRI SAT

Top three focuses today

1. _____

2. _____

3. _____

What's got you stressed?   Now let it go.

What are you **grateful** for?

Water

Don't-Forgets!

Morning

Notes

Mid-Day

Evening

Date: _____   SUN MON TUE WED THU FRI SAT

Top three focuses today

1. _____

2. _____

3. _____

What's got you stressed?   Now let it go.

What are you **grateful** for?

Water

Don't-Forgets!

Morning

Notes

Mid-Day

Evening

SUNDAY	MONDAY	TUESDAY	WEDNESDAY
_____	_____	_____	_____
_____	_____	_____	_____
_____	_____	_____	_____
_____	_____	_____	_____
_____	_____	_____	_____

THURSDAY	FRIDAY	SATURDAY	NOTES
_____	_____	_____	
_____	_____	_____	
_____	_____	_____	
_____	_____	_____	
_____	_____	_____	

MONTH

REVIEW

Look back on the last 30 days and answer the following:

What was fun, fulfilling, or just worked really, really well?

What could have gone better? No judgment, simply a chance to reflect.

What do you want to make more time for next month?
What do you want to spend less time doing?

What areas of life in the past 30 days felt too complicated?
Where could you benefit from less chaos?

How can you simplify these areas in the next 30 days?

PLAN

What two things do you want to focus on during the next 30 days?

1.

2.

What are you procrastinating on right now? Is this because of fear or lack of skill?

How are you going to overcome this?

What steps do you need to take in order to implement your answers from the previous page? Get those things on (or off) the calendar for next month.

Review your Goals & Visions pages. Make sure the steps you need to be taking are scheduled. If you need to adjust the timeline on your goals, now is the time.

Go forth and conquer the next 30 days.

Date: _____   SUN MON TUE WED THU FRI SAT

Top three focuses today

1. _____

2. _____

3. _____

What's got you stressed?   Now let it go.

What are you **grateful** for?

Water

Don't-Forgets!

Morning

Notes

Mid-Day

Evening

Date: _____   SUN MON TUE WED THU FRI SAT

Top three focuses today

1. _____

2. _____

3. _____

What's got you stressed?	Now let it go.

What are you **grateful** for?

Water

Don't-Forgets!

Morning

Notes

Mid-Day

Evening

Date: _____   SUN MON TUE WED THU FRI SAT

Top three focuses today

1. _____

2. _____

3. _____

What's got you stressed?   Now let it go.

What are you **grateful** for?

Water   **Don't-Forgets!**

Morning

Notes

Mid-Day

Evening

Date: _____   SUN MON TUE WED THU FRI SAT

Top three focuses today

1. _____

2. _____

3. _____

What's got you stressed?   Now let it go.

What are you **grateful** for?

Water

Don't-Forgets!

Morning

Notes

Mid-Day

Evening

Date: _____   SUN MON TUE WED THU FRI SAT

Top three focuses today

1. _____

2. _____

3. _____

What's got you stressed?   Now let it go.

What are you **grateful** for?

Water   **Don't-Forgets!**

Morning

Notes

Mid-Day

Evening

Date: _____   SUN MON TUE WED THU FRI SAT

Top three focuses today

1. _____

2. _____

3. _____

What's got you stressed?	Now let it go.

What are you **grateful** for?

Water	Don't-Forgets!

Morning

Notes

Mid-Day

Evening

Date: _____   SUN MON TUE WED THU FRI SAT

Top three focuses today

1. _____

2. _____

3. _____

| What's got you stressed? | Now let it go. |

What are you **grateful** for?

Water

Don't-Forgets!

Morning

Notes

Mid-Day

Evening

Date: _____   SUN MON TUE WED THU FRI SAT

Top three focuses today

1. _____

2. _____

3. _____

What's got you stressed?	Now let it go.

What are you **grateful** for?

Water	Don't-Forgets!

Morning

Notes

Mid-Day

Evening

Date: _____   SUN MON TUE WED THU FRI SAT

Top three focuses today

1. _____

2. _____

3. _____

What's got you stressed?   Now let it go.

What are you **grateful** for?

Water

Don't-Forgets!

Morning

Notes

Mid-Day

Evening

Date: _____   SUN MON TUE WED THU FRI SAT

Top three focuses today

1. _____

2. _____

3. _____

What's got you stressed?   Now let it go.

What are you **grateful** for?

Water

Don't-Forgets!

Morning

Notes

Mid-Day

Evening

Date: _____   SUN MON TUE WED THU FRI SAT

Top three focuses today

1. _____

2. _____

3. _____

What's got you stressed?	Now let it go.

What are you **grateful** for?

Water

Don't-Forgets!

Morning

Notes

Mid-Day

Evening

Date: _____   SUN MON TUE WED THU FRI SAT

Top three focuses today

1. _____

2. _____

3. _____

What's got you stressed?   Now let it go.

What are you **grateful** for?

Water

Don't-Forgets!

Morning

Notes

Mid-Day

Evening

Date: _____   SUN MON TUE WED THU FRI SAT

Top three focuses today

1. _____

2. _____

3. _____

What's got you stressed?   Now let it go.

What are you **grateful** for?

Water

Don't-Forgets!

Morning

Notes

Mid-Day

Evening

Date: _____ SUN MON TUE WED THU FRI SAT

Top three focuses today

1. _____

2. _____

3. _____

What's got you stressed?   Now let it go.

What are you **grateful** for?

Water

Don't-Forgets!

Morning

Notes

Mid-Day

Evening

Date: _____   SUN MON TUE WED THU FRI SAT

Top three focuses today

1. _____

2. _____

3. _____

What's got you stressed?   Now let it go.

What are you **grateful** for?

Water

Don't-Forgets!

Morning

Notes

Mid-Day

Evening

Date: _____   SUN MON TUE WED THU FRI SAT

Top three focuses today

1. _____

2. _____

3. _____

What's got you stressed?   Now let it go.

What are you **grateful** for?

Water

Don't-Forgets!

Morning

Notes

Mid-Day

Evening

Date: _____   SUN MON TUE WED THU FRI SAT

Top three focuses today

1. _____

2. _____

3. _____

What's got you stressed?   Now let it go.

What are you **grateful** for?

Water

Don't-Forgets!

Morning

Notes

Mid-Day

Evening

Date: _____

Top three focuses today

1. _____

2. _____

3. _____

What's got you stressed?	Now let it go.

What are you **grateful** for?

Water

Don't-Forgets!

Morning

Notes

Mid-Day

Evening

Date: _____   SUN MON TUE WED THU FRI SAT

Top three focuses today

1. _____

2. _____

3. _____

| What's got you stressed? | Now let it go. |

What are you **grateful** for?

Water

Don't-Forgets!

Morning

Notes

Mid-Day

Evening

Date: _____   SUN MON TUE WED THU FRI SAT

Top three focuses today

1. _____

2. _____

3. _____

What's got you stressed?   Now let it go.

What are you **grateful** for?

Water

Don't-Forgets!

Morning

Notes

Mid-Day

Evening

Date: _____   SUN MON TUE WED THU FRI SAT

Top three focuses today

1. _____

2. _____

3. _____

What's got you stressed?   Now let it go.

What are you **grateful** for?

Water

Don't-Forgets!

Morning

Notes

Mid-Day

Evening

Date: _____ SUN MON TUE WED THU FRI SAT

Top three focuses today

1. _____

2. _____

3. _____

What's got you stressed?   Now let it go.

What are you **grateful** for?

Water

Don't-Forgets!

Morning

Notes

Mid-Day

Evening

Date: _____   SUN MON TUE WED THU FRI SAT

Top three focuses today

1. _____

2. _____

3. _____

What's got you stressed?   Now let it go.

What are you **grateful** for?

Water

Don't-Forgets!

Morning

Notes

Mid-Day

Evening

Date: _____   SUN MON TUE WED THU FRI SAT

Top three focuses today

1. _____

2. _____

3. _____

What's got you stressed?   Now let it go.

What are you **grateful** for?

Water

Don't-Forgets!

Morning

Notes

Mid-Day

Evening

Date: _____   SUN MON TUE WED THU FRI SAT

Top three focuses today

1. _____

2. _____

3. _____

What's got you stressed?   Now let it go.

What are you **grateful** for?

Water

Don't-Forgets!

Morning

Notes

Mid-Day

Evening

Date: _____   SUN MON TUE WED THU FRI SAT

Top three focuses today

1. _____

2. _____

3. _____

What's got you stressed?	Now let it go.

What are you **grateful** for?

Water

Don't-Forgets!

Morning

Notes

Mid-Day

Evening

Date: _____   SUN MON TUE WED THU FRI SAT

Top three focuses today

1. _____

2. _____

3. _____

What's got you stressed?	Now let it go.

What are you **grateful** for?

Water

Don't-Forgets!

Morning

Notes

Mid-Day

Evening

Date: _____   SUN MON TUE WED THU FRI SAT

Top three focuses today

1. _____

2. _____

3. _____

What's got you stressed?   Now let it go.

What are you **grateful** for?

Water

Don't-Forgets!

Morning

Notes

Mid-Day

Evening

Date: _____   SUN MON TUE WED THU FRI SAT

Top three focuses today

1. _____

2. _____

3. _____

What's got you stressed?   Now let it go.

What are you **grateful** for?

Water	Don't-Forgets!

Morning

Notes

Mid-Day

Evening

Date: _____   SUN MON TUE WED THU FRI SAT

Top three focuses today

1. _____

2. _____

3. _____

What's got you stressed?   Now let it go.

What are you **grateful** for?

Water

Don't-Forgets!

Morning

Notes

Mid-Day

Evening

Date: _____   SUN MON TUE WED THU FRI SAT

Top three focuses today

1. _____

2. _____

3. _____

| What's got you stressed? | Now let it go. |

What are you **grateful** for?

Water

Don't-Forgets!

Morning

Notes

Mid-Day

Evening

SUNDAY	MONDAY	TUESDAY	WEDNESDAY	
_____	_____	_____	_____	
_____	_____	_____	_____	
_____	_____	_____	_____	
_____	_____	_____	_____	
_____	_____	_____	_____	

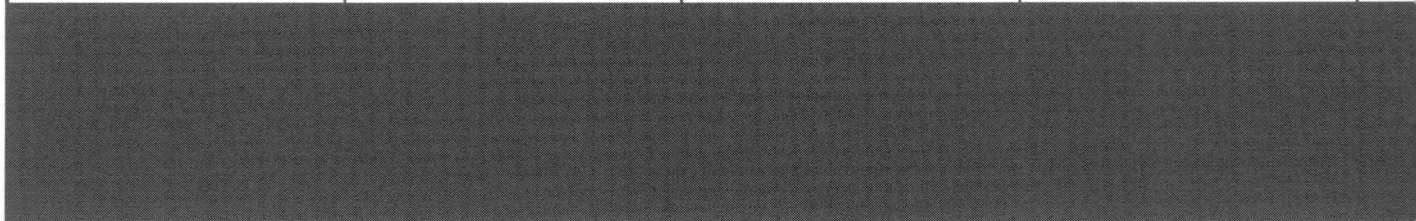

THURSDAY	FRIDAY	SATURDAY	NOTES
___	___	___	
___	___	___	
___	___	___	
___	___	___	
___	___	___	

MONTH

REVIEW

Look back on the last 30 days and answer the following:

What was fun, fulfilling, or just worked really, really well?

What could have gone better? No judgment, simply a chance to reflect.

What do you want to make more time for next month?
What do you want to spend less time doing?

What areas of life in the past 30 days felt too complicated?
Where could you benefit from less chaos?

How can you simplify these areas in the next 30 days?

PLAN

What two things do you want to focus on during the next 30 days?

1.

2.

What are you procrastinating on right now? Is this because of fear or lack of skill?

How are you going to overcome this?

What steps do you need to take in order to implement your answers from the previous page? Get those things on (or off) the calendar for next month.

Review your Goals & Visions pages. Make sure the steps you need to be taking are scheduled. If you need to adjust the timeline on your goals, now is the time.

Go forth and conquer the next 30 days.

Date: _____   SUN MON TUE WED THU FRI SAT

Top three focuses today

1. _____

2. _____

3. _____

What's got you stressed?   Now let it go.

What are you **grateful** for?

Water

Don't-Forgets!

Morning

Notes

Mid-Day

Evening

Date: _____   SUN MON TUE WED THU FRI SAT

Top three focuses today

1. _____

2. _____

3. _____

What's got you stressed?   Now let it go.

What are you **grateful** for?

Water

Don't-Forgets!

Morning

Notes

Mid-Day

Evening

Date: _____   SUN MON TUE WED THU FRI SAT

Top three focuses today

1. _____

2. _____

3. _____

What's got you stressed?	Now let it go.

What are you **grateful** for?

Water	**Don't-Forgets!**

Morning

Notes

Mid-Day

Evening

Date: _____   SUN MON TUE WED THU FRI SAT

Top three focuses today

1. _____

2. _____

3. _____

What's got you stressed?	Now let it go.

What are you **grateful** for?

Water

Don't-Forgets!

Morning

Notes

Mid-Day

Evening

Date: _____   SUN MON TUE WED THU FRI SAT

Top three focuses today

1. _____

2. _____

3. _____

What's got you stressed?   Now let it go.

What are you **grateful** for?

Water

Don't-Forgets!

Morning

Notes

Mid-Day

Evening

Date: _____   SUN MON TUE WED THU FRI SAT

Top three focuses today

1. _____

2. _____

3. _____

What's got you stressed?   Now let it go.

What are you **grateful** for?

Water

Don't-Forgets!

Morning

Notes

Mid-Day

Evening

Date: _____   SUN MON TUE WED THU FRI SAT

Top three focuses today

1. _____

2. _____

3. _____

What's got you stressed?	Now let it go.

What are you **grateful** for?

Water

Don't-Forgets!

Morning

Notes

Mid-Day

Evening

Date: _____   SUN MON TUE WED THU FRI SAT

Top three focuses today

1. _____

2. _____

3. _____

What's got you stressed?   Now let it go.

What are you **grateful** for?

Water

Don't-Forgets!

Morning

Notes

Mid-Day

Evening

Date: _____ SUN MON TUE WED THU FRI SAT

Top three focuses today

1. _____

2. _____

3. _____

What's got you stressed?   Now let it go.

What are you **grateful** for?

Water

Don't-Forgets!

Morning

Notes

Mid-Day

Evening

Date: _____   SUN MON TUE WED THU FRI SAT

Top three focuses today

1. _____

2. _____

3. _____

What's got you stressed?   Now let it go.

What are you **grateful** for?

Water

Don't-Forgets!

Morning

Notes

Mid-Day

Evening

Date: _____   SUN MON TUE WED THU FRI SAT

Top three focuses today

1. _____

2. _____

3. _____

| What's got you stressed? | Now let it go. |

What are you **grateful** for?

Water

Don't-Forgets!

Morning

Notes

Mid-Day

Evening

Date: _____   SUN MON TUE WED THU FRI SAT

Top three focuses today

1. _____

2. _____

3. _____

What's got you stressed?   Now let it go.

What are you **grateful** for?

Water

Don't-Forgets!

Morning

Notes

Mid-Day

Evening

Date: _____

SUN MON TUE WED THU FRI SAT

Top three focuses today

1. _____

2. _____

3. _____

What's got you stressed?   Now let it go.

What are you **grateful** for?

Water

Don't-Forgets!

Morning

Notes

Mid-Day

Evening

Date: _____   SUN MON TUE WED THU FRI SAT

Top three focuses today

1. _____

2. _____

3. _____

What's got you stressed?   Now let it go.

What are you **grateful** for?

Water

Don't-Forgets!

Morning

Notes

Mid-Day

Evening

Date: _____   SUN MON TUE WED THU FRI SAT

Top three focuses today

1. _____

2. _____

3. _____

| What's got you stressed? | Now let it go. |

What are you **grateful** for?

Water

Don't-Forgets!

Morning

Notes

Mid-Day

Evening

Date: _____   SUN MON TUE WED THU FRI SAT

Top three focuses today

1. _____

2. _____

3. _____

What's got you stressed?   Now let it go.

What are you **grateful** for?

Water

Don't-Forgets!

Morning

Notes

Mid-Day

Evening

Date: _____   SUN MON TUE WED THU FRI SAT

Top three focuses today

1. _____

2. _____

3. _____

What's got you stressed?   Now let it go.

What are you **grateful** for?

Water

Don't-Forgets!

Morning

Notes

Mid-Day

Evening

Date: _____   SUN MON TUE WED THU FRI SAT

Top three focuses today

1. _____

2. _____

3. _____

What's got you stressed?   Now let it go.

What are you **grateful** for?

Water

Don't-Forgets!

Morning

Notes

Mid-Day

Evening

Date: _____   SUN MON TUE WED THU FRI SAT

Top three focuses today

1. _____

2. _____

3. _____

What's got you stressed?   Now let it go.

What are you **grateful** for?

Water

Don't-Forgets!

Morning

Notes

Mid-Day

Evening

Date: _____   SUN MON TUE WED THU FRI SAT

Top three focuses today

1. _____

2. _____

3. _____

What's got you stressed?   Now let it go.

What are you **grateful** for?

Water

Don't-Forgets!

Morning

Notes

Mid-Day

Evening

Date: _____   SUN MON TUE WED THU FRI SAT

Top three focuses today

1. _____

2. _____

3. _____

What's got you stressed?   Now let it go.

What are you **grateful** for?

Water

Don't-Forgets!

Morning

Notes

Mid-Day

Evening

Date: _____   SUN MON TUE WED THU FRI SAT

Top three focuses today

1. _____

2. _____

3. _____

What's got you stressed?   Now let it go.

What are you **grateful** for?

Water

Don't-Forgets!

Morning

Notes

Mid-Day

Evening

Date: _____   SUN MON TUE WED THU FRI SAT

Top three focuses today

1. _____

2. _____

3. _____

What's got you stressed?   Now let it go.

What are you **grateful** for?

Water

Don't-Forgets!

Morning   Notes

Mid-Day

Evening

Date: _____

Top three focuses today

1. _____

2. _____

3. _____

What's got you stressed?	Now let it go.

What are you **grateful** for?

Water	**Don't-Forgets!**

Morning

Notes

Mid-Day

Evening

Date: _____   SUN MON TUE WED THU FRI SAT

Top three focuses today

1. _____

2. _____

3. _____

What's got you stressed?	Now let it go.

What are you **grateful** for?

Water

Don't-Forgets!

Morning

Notes

Mid-Day

Evening

Date: _____   SUN MON TUE WED THU FRI SAT

Top three focuses today

1. _____

2. _____

3. _____

What's got you stressed?   Now let it go.

What are you **grateful** for?

Water

Don't-Forgets!

Morning

Notes

Mid-Day

Evening

Date: _____   SUN MON TUE WED THU FRI SAT

Top three focuses today

1. _____

2. _____

3. _____

What's got you stressed?	Now let it go.

What are you **grateful** for?

Water	**Don't-Forgets!**

Morning

Notes

Mid-Day

Evening

Date: _____   SUN MON TUE WED THU FRI SAT

Top three focuses today

1. _____

2. _____

3. _____

What's got you stressed?	Now let it go.

What are you **grateful** for?

Water	**Don't-Forgets!**

Morning   Notes

Mid-Day

Evening

Date: _____   SUN MON TUE WED THU FRI SAT

Top three focuses today

1. _____

2. _____

3. _____

What's got you stressed?   Now let it go.

What are you **grateful** for?

Water

Don't-Forgets!

Morning

Notes

Mid-Day

Evening

Date: _____   SUN MON TUE WED THU FRI SAT

Top three focuses today

1. _____

2. _____

3. _____

What's got you stressed?   Now let it go.

What are you **grateful** for?

Water

Don't-Forgets!

Morning   Notes

_____

_____

_____

_____

_____

_____

Mid-Day

_____

_____

_____

_____

_____

_____

Evening

_____

_____

_____

_____

_____

_____

Date: _____   SUN MON TUE WED THU FRI SAT

Top three focuses today

1. _____

2. _____

3. _____

What's got you stressed?   Now let it go.

What are you **grateful** for?

Water

Don't-Forgets!

Morning

Notes

Mid-Day

Evening

KEEP KICKING ASS & TAKING NAMES

I truly hope that the past 12 weeks have been full of success and growth, and that this day tracker helped bring it all together.

I'd love to hear from you!

hello@caseyjourdan.com
Twitter - @caseyjourdan
Instagram - @livefullproject

Tell me of your success.
Let me know what you loved about the Life-Hacking Day Tracker and if there are any areas I can improve for future editions.

47182621R00121

Made in the USA
San Bernardino, CA
24 March 2017